WE ARE NEIGHBORS! BEING A PART OF COMMUNITY

Social Skills Book Kindergarten

Children's Friendship & Social Skills Books

Speedy Publishing LLC

40 E. Main St. #1156

Newark, DE 19711

www.speedypublishing.com

Copyright 2017

Unless you live all by yourself on an island or in a cave, you probably have neighbors. How do you be a good neighbor to them? Let's find out.

WHAT IS A NEIGHBOR?

Think of the people who live on your street, and on the next street over, and on the street after that. Those are some of your neighbors. They help make where you live the way it is. Good neighbors help make where you live a good place. Bad neighbors...well, you don't want to have bad neighbors. And you certainly don't want to be a bad neighbor to others!

The people closest to you in the world are your family, both the people you live with and family members whom you see when they come to visit, or on holidays. They are your closest circle.

FAMILY HAVING A BIG DINNER TOGETHER AT HOME

Your next circle is your good friends. You know them well, you like to play with them, and even if you fight with them you still like them afterwards.

The next circle out is your neighbors. They live, work, and go to school with you, but they aren't part of your family. There are so many that you probably don't know all their names.

A WOMAN TALKING WITH HER NEIGHBOR

GIRL WATCHING MOVIE ON TELEVISION IN LIVING ROOM

Beyond them are all the people you don't know yet. They may be famous people you see on television or in movies, so you know a lot about them. They may be people who live so far away and speak such a different language that you will never get to know them.

You know your family and your friends really well. It's very hard to know the people who live far away. But do you know your neighbors, the people who live nearby? What do they like? How could you make their life better?.

UNITY AND FRIENDSHIP OF NEIGHBORS

JEREMIAH 32:20
HOLY
BIBLE

WHAT MAKES A GOOD NEIGHBOR?

In the Bible, Jesus told people they should love their neighbors the way they love themselves. Somebody in the crowd asked, "Yeah, but who is my neighbor?" It was like he was trying to figure out how few people he would have to love.

Jesus answered by telling a story. In our world today, it would go something like this:

There was man who had some business to do. He was going from one city to another city, walking along the road. Some robbers attacked him and beat him up. They stole what he had, hurt him badly, and left him lying on the side of the road.

ROBBER

VICTIM LYING ON STREET

The man lay there on the road, bleeding. He needed help! Who would help him?

Fortunately, a lawyer came along the road. He saw the man lying on the ground, he saw that the man was in trouble—but he walked right by. He didn't want to get involved.

The a minister came along the road. Perhaps he was in a hurry to go visit some members of his congregation. Perhaps he didn't want to get his nice clothes all yucky while helping the man lying in the road. But for whatever reason, he even crossed the street so he could go past that man at a safe distance.

Would nobody help the man?

BUSY MAN CHECKING TIME WHILE WALKING

MAN WITH EMERGENCY CALL ON HIS SMARTPHONE
911
EMERGENCY CALL

Finally, a stranger to the area came along the road. He saw the man. He didn't know him; he had never seen the man before.

But the stranger stopped. He turned the man over to make sure he was breathing. He used handkerchiefs to slow down the worst bleeding. And he called the emergency number on his cell phone to get an ambulance to come.

But the ambulance didn't come for a while. So the stranger got the wounded man into his own car—never mind about the blood on the seat!—and drove him to the nearest hospital.

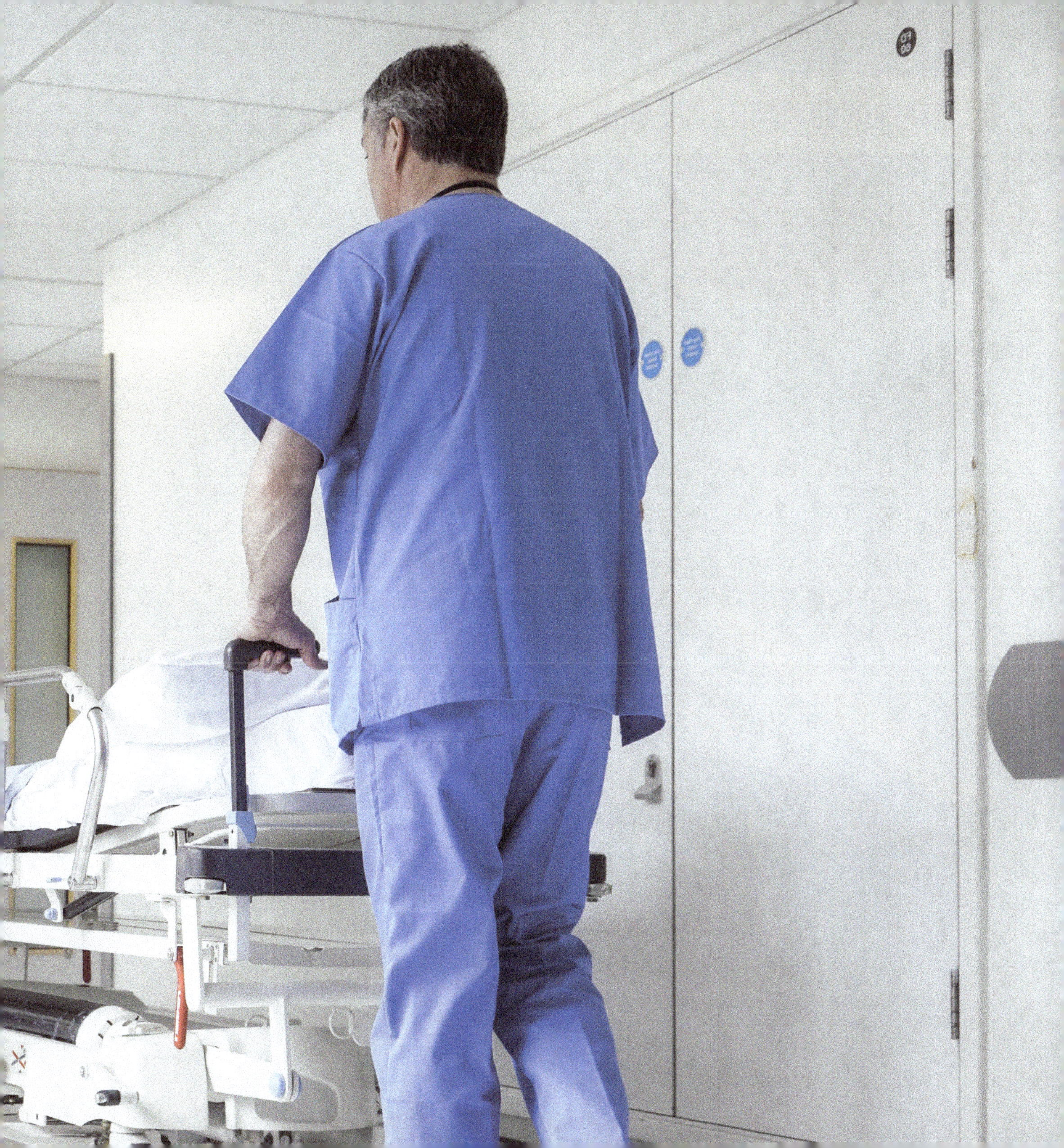

MAN GIVING CREDIT CARD FROM WALLET

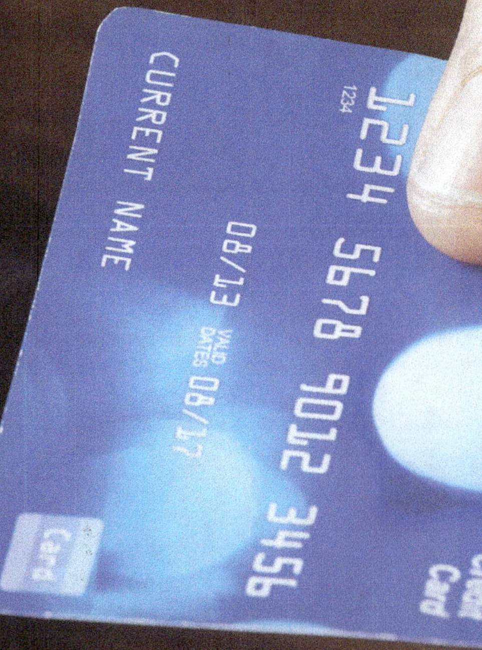

At the hospital the people weren't sure if the man had health insurance, because he was unconscious and his wallet had been stolen. So the stranger hauled out his own credit card and said, "Look, if he has no insurance, put the charges on my card."

When the story was over, Jesus asked the man who had asked about neighbors, "What do you think? Who was the neighbor of that man who was attacked and hurt?"

The man who had asked the question thought about it and finally said, "I guess the guy who helped him was like a neighbor to him. But—"

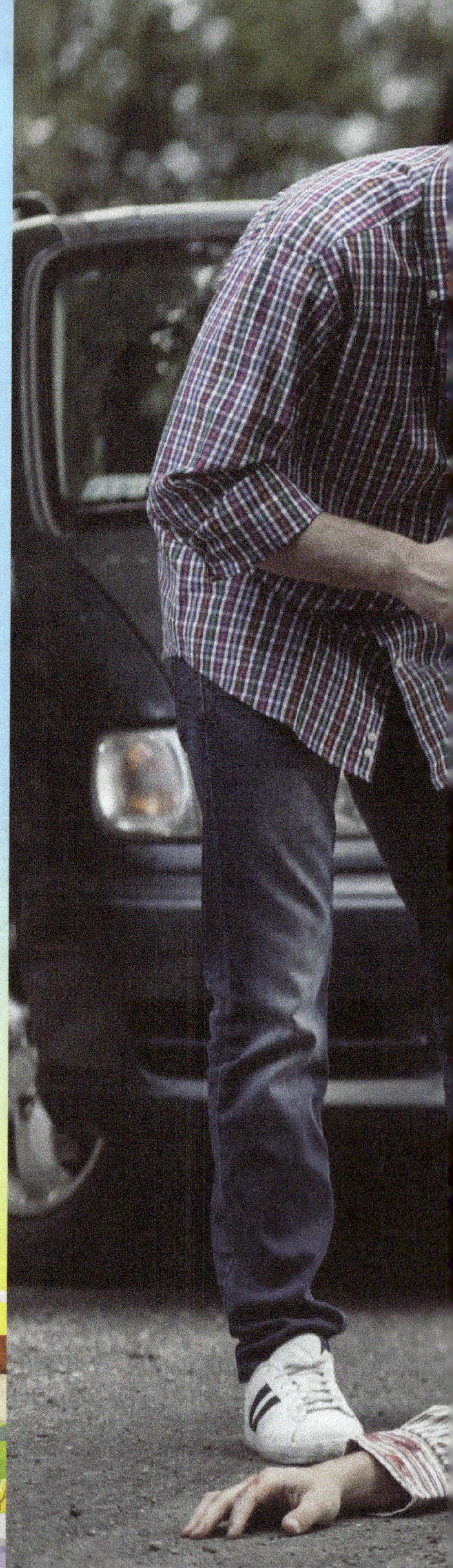

A WOMAN HELPING AN ELDER CROSS THE STREET

nd Jesus said, "There you go: if you want to show that you're a neighbor, that's the sort of stuff you do. And that's the sort of stuff you would like others to do for you."

What Jesus was saying was that, in the end, it doesn't matter as much how close people live to you, if you want to know if you and they are neighbors. How you act toward them shows whether you are their neighbor.

HOW TO BE NEIGHBORLY

Here are some ideas for how to be a good neighbor for the people you run into around where you live, even if they have not been attacked by robbers!

- **KNOW THEIR NAMES.** Do you know the names of the people living in the houses around your house? Do you know what they like to be called? People really like it when you know their names and know to call them "Dr. Smith" or "Mrs. Smith".

COUPLE STANDING OUTSIDE TALKING TO A NEW NEIGHBOR

A BEAUTIFUL AND NEATLY GROOMED HOME

- **THINK OF THEIR EYES.** If you can look at your neighbors, they can look back at you. If you have a front yard, it is nice to keep it neat so your neighbors can look out their windows at a pretty street scene. It doesn't mean you can't play in your yard, or even make a mess with sidewalk chalk or water balloons. Just remember to clean up when you are done!

- **THINK OF THEIR EARS.** There are times for noise, and there are times for quiet. Your neighbors probably like hearing kids playing outside during the day, after school.

GROUP OF LITTLE CHILDREN SITTING ON STONE STAIRS TO THE HOUSE DOOR

MOTHER PUTTING BABY TO SLEEP IN THE CRIB

They are probably less happy if there is a lot of running and screaming after dark, when they are trying to put their small children to sleep. In the same way, even if your neighbors like to listen to their own music, it doesn't mean they want to listen to your music.

If you want to hear your music at a high volume, take it indoors or put in ear buds (but then still don't play the music so high that you hurt your ears!).

CUTE LITTLE GIRL WEARING HUGE WIRELESS HEADPHONES

THREE CHILDREN PUTTING ITEMS INTO RECYCLE BIN

- **THINK OF THEIR NEEDS.** You don't have to mow your neighbor's lawn. But if somebody dumped a coffee cup or some other junk on their lawn, you could go pick it up and put it in the garbage. You don't even have to tell them you did it!

- **THINK OF THEIR FEARS.**
You may have a nice, friendly dog, but your neighbors may not be sure the dog is friendly. Keep the dog on a leash when it is not in your yard, so it does not scare any of your neighbors.

CAVALIER KING CHARGES SPANIEL GOING FOR A WALK

FAMILY ENJOYING CHINESE MEAL

- **CONSIDER THEIR CUSTOMS.** Not everybody lives the way you live. Other families have different patterns for when and what they eat, when their kids can come out to play, even if boys and girls can talk to each other. Listen and learn: your way of life is not wrong and their way of life is not wrong, even if they don't match in some ways. See if you can find other ways where you and they agree, and don't worry so much about the differences.

WHEN NEW PEOPLE MOVE IN

People come and go. Sometimes new people move into your neighborhood. What should you do to show you are their neighbor?

- **INTRODUCE YOURSELF.** When you meet them outside their house, greet them and say who you are. Point to where you live. Tell them you are happy they have joined the neighborhood.

WOMAN TALKING TO AN ELDERLY MALE NEIGHBOR

GARBAGE COLLECTOR

- **LEARN THEIR NAMES.** Did we say that before? It's still true!

- **HELP THEM LEARN THE NEIGHBORHOOD.** Do they know what day the garbage is collected? Do they know when the community center shows the free movies? You don't have to drown them in information, but it is nice to share a few things about where you and they both live.

- **WHAT CAN THEY TEACH YOU?** Did they just move to town from Greenland? Without annoying them, ask what it was like to live in their old town.

THE COLORFUL HOUSES OF RODEBAY, GREENLAND.

If they cook different kinds of food from you, don't wrinkle your nose at the new smells. Instead, ask what the recipe is and how they learned to make it.

If they are from another country, can you learn how they say common phrases, like "Hello," "Goodbye," and "Have a nice day"?

ao
Hello
Hola
вет
Hallo
Bonjour

HOW PEOPLE LIVE

People in different parts of the world, and at different times in history, have followed different customs. Those customs develop because of where in the world the people live, what they believe (and what they fear!), and what resources they have on hand. Learn about the daily life of people in very different places and times in these Baby Professor books: The Daily Life of a Mayan Family, The Daily Life of Muslims During the Largest Empire in History, The Daily Life of a Roman Family in the Ancient Times, and The Daily Struggles of Those who Lived in the Middle Ages.

Visit
BABY PROFESSOR
EDUCATION KIDS
www.BabyProfessorBooks.com
to download Free Baby Professor eBooks
and view our catalog of new and exciting
Children's Books